Introduction

contents contents

introduction

Nothing beats the taste of home-baked cakes and biscuits. Yet, today many people think of home-baked goodies as nothing more than a delightful memory. This need not be so. This book will show that not only is baking an easy and affordable way to fill lunch boxes and provide snacks for your family, but it is also fun. Here you will find a host of recipes that are easy to make and will bring those distant memories of freshly-baked treats back to life. Baking has never been simpler or more fun than with this selection of quick and easy cakes and bakes. A bowl, a beater and a few minutes in the kitchen is all it takes to fill the house with the homey warmth and aroma that only a homemade muffin, cake or batch of biscuits can provide. There's a

recipe in these pages to please everyone and every occasion. So, discover the pleasure of home baking and watch your friends and family return for more.

Muffins

The perfect muffin has a gently rounded top and golden crust, moist finely-grained crumb, an appealing aroma and a satisfying balance of flavour.

Muffins are mini-cakes for busy home bakers – freeze them for brunch treats, quick snacks and school lunch boxes, or when you need to stop and take a well-earned break.

Quick breads, true to their name.

are quick and easy to bake. They use baking powder or bicarbonate of soda instead of yeast as the rising agent. In this chapter, you will find recipes for such delicious quick breads as bacon-cornbread pots, herb rolls, and carrot and sesame muffins.

Techniques

When adding fresh fruit to batter it is best to follow the following advice: Whole berries and chopped fresh fruit are less likely to sink to the bottom of muffins and other quick breads during baking if you dredge them in flour first. Then shake off the excess flour in a colander before adding them to the batter. Besides helping to suspend the fruit evenly throughout the batter, the flour coating keeps moist pieces of fruit from clumping together. The basic ingredients in muffins – flour, flavourings, perhaps some leavening, and liquid – are the same ones used in almost a dozen other varieties of quick breads.

Creating such amazing diversity from a few common staples is largely a matter of adjusting the proportions of dry and liquid ingredients. Use two parts dry to one part liquid ingredients and you get a thicker batter for baking muffins or loaves. Thicker still, with a ratio of dry to liquid ingredients approaching three to one, are soft doughs for cut biscuits and scones. Muffins and most quick breads are at their best when eaten soon after baking. Those that contain fruit, nuts, vegetables or moderately high amounts of fat stay moist longer than those that are low in fat. If muffins are left over it is best to place in the freezer in an airtight container, where they will keep for up to twelve months. To reheat, bake the frozen muffins, wrapped in foil, at 175°C/350°F for 15-20 minutes, or until heated through. You may also store quick breads and biscuits in the same manner.

sweet
muffins

oatbran

and fruit muffin

170g/6oz plain flour

1 tsp baking powder

30g/1oz oat bran

75g/2¹/₂oz brown sugar

115mL/4fl oz canola oil

2 eggs

115g/4oz fruit medley

1 cup buttermilk

1 Combine flour, baking powder, oat bran and brown sugar. Beat oil and eggs together and stir in the dry ingredients along with the fruit medley and buttermilk. Mix until just combined, do not over mix.

2 Spoon mixture into lightly greased muffin pans. Bake in an oven 190°C/375°F/Gas Mark 5 for 25-30 minutes.

***Makes** 10 **Preparation** 10mins **Cooking** 30mins
Calories 281 each **Fat** 2g each*

raspberry

and white

1 Preheat the oven to 150°C/300°F/Gas Mark 2.

2 In a small saucepan, melt the butter, coffee granules and hot water together (until smooth) and then remove from the heat.

3 Add the cooking chocolate and superfine sugar, and stir thoroughly (until the chocolate has dissolved).

4 Sift together the flour, baking powder and cocoa, then add to the liquid chocolate mixture and mix well. Whisk the eggs and vanilla, then add to the chocolate mixture.

5 Prepare 10-12 muffin cups (or 2 trays of 6 cups each) by lightly buttering them, then dusting lightly with flour. Tip out the excess. Place 2 tablespoons of batter into each of the muffin cups, then add a spoonful of white chocolate and some raspberries to the centre of each muffin cup. Divide the remaining chocolate batter between the muffin cups and tap gently to settle the mixture.

6 Bake for 20 minutes (or until firm on top when touched). When baked, remove the cakes from the oven and allow to cool in the pan for 5 minutes. Then carefully loosen each little cake from the pan. Turn the muffin tray upside down on a flat surface to remove.

7 Meanwhile, make the sauce. Heat the cream (until boiling), then pour it over the chocolate pieces that have been broken up and placed in a heatproof bowl. Allow the cream and chocolate to sit for 10 minutes, then gently, but thoroughly, stir the mixture. Add the coffee liqueur and stir again (until smooth).

8 To serve, drizzle the chocolate sauce over the plate, then carefully place each cake in the centre of the plates. Add some thick cream (or vanilla-bean ice cream) and serve.

9 *Variation: If raspberries are not in season, use chopped dried apricots or fresh orange segments (drained) and substitute Grand Marnier for the coffee liqueur.*

chocolate-filled muffins

For Cake

255g/9oz butter

1 tsp instant-coffee granules

1 1/2 cups hot water

200g/7oz cooking chocolate

2 cups superfine sugar

1 1/2 cups plain flour

1/2 tsp baking powder

1/4 cup Dutch cocoa

2 eggs

2 tsp vanilla

85g/3oz white chocolate (chopped finely)

115g/4oz raspberries

For Sauce

1 cup cream

1 cup quality chocolate

2 tbsp Kahlua coffee liqueur

spiced
apple muffins

1 Preheat the oven to 200°C/400°F/Gas Mark 6. Line a muffin or deep bun pan with 9 muffin cases and set aside. Place the flour, baking powder, mixed spice and salt in a bowl and mix well.

2 In a separate large bowl, mix together the sugar, egg, milk and the melted sunflower spread, then gently fold in the flour mixture, just enough to combine them. (The mixture should look quite lumpy; it will produce heavy muffins if overmixed.) Gently fold in the apple.

3 Divide the mixture between the muffin cases. Bake in the oven for 20 minutes or until risen and golden brown. Transfer to a wire rack to cool.

Cooking apples contain useful amounts of vitamin C, while both eating apples and cooking apples are a good source of soluble fibre which can help to reduce cholesterol levels.

200g/7oz plain wholemeal flour

1 tbsp baking powder

1½ tsp ground mixed spice

pinch of salt

2oz/55g light soft brown sugar

1 medium egg, beaten

200mL/7fl oz half-fat milk

55g/2oz sunflower spread, melted

1 cooking apple, peeled, cored and chopped

Serves makes 9 muffins   **Preparation** 20mins
Cooking 20mins   **Calories** 161 each   **Fat** 6g each

strawberry

filled muffins

510g/18oz plain flour

55g/2oz sugar

3 tsp baking powder

$1/2$ tsp salt

$1/8$ tsp ground nutmeg

I egg

255mL/9fl oz milk

3 tbsp butter, melted
and cooled, or oil

85g/3oz strawberry
jelly

Serves *makes 12 muffins*
Preparation *15mins*
Cooking *25mins*
Calories *160 each*
Fat *3g each*

I Preheat the oven to 200°C/400°F/Gas Mark 6. In a large bowl stir together flour, sugar, baking powder, salt, and nutmeg. Make well in centre.

2 In a medium bowl beat egg with milk and melted butter. Pour egg mixture, stirring just until dry ingredients are moistened.

3 Fill prepared muffins pans about one-third full, using half the batter. To each muffin cup, add about 1 teaspoon strawberry jelly. Use remaining batter to fill pans two-thirds full.

4 Bake until well browned (20-25 minutes). Serve warm.

fig pudding

with butterscotch sauce

255g/9oz dried figs, chopped

255mL/9fl oz water

1 tsp baking soda

2 eggs

2oz/55g butter

6½oz/185g superfine sugar

185g/6½oz plain flour

½ tsp baking powder

1 vanilla bean

1 tsp vanilla essence

Butterscotch Sauce

1 cup brown sugar

200mL/7fl oz cream

30g/1oz unsalted butter

cream or ice cream, for serving

1 Preheat oven to 190°C/375°F/Gas Mark 5.

2 Place the figs, water and baking soda in a saucepan, and cook for about 20 minutes, or until mixture has reached a jelly-consistency.

3 Pour the fig mixture into a bowl, and beat in the remaining ingredients. Split the vanilla bean down middle, scrape out the seeds, and add them to the mixture.

4 Pour mixture into individual ramekins or timbale-moulds, and bake in the oven for 25 minutes.

5 To make the sauce: Combine all the ingredients in a saucepan, and stir over a low heat, until dissolved.

6 Serve the individual puddings with the sauce and cream, or ice cream.

Serves 6   *Preparation* 35mins   *Cooking* 1hr   *Calories* 595 each   *Fat* 8g each

banana

choc-chip muffins

1 large ripe banana
9fl oz/255mL milk
1 egg
2oz/55g margarine, melted
6½oz/185g plain flour
½ tsp baking powder
4oz/115g superfine sugar
4oz/115g choc bits

1 In a mixing bowl mash the banana, add the milk, egg and melted margarine. Mix well.

2 Stir the flour, baking powder, sugar and choc bits into the banana mixture, mix only until the ingredients are combined.

3 Spoon mixture into well greased muffin tins. Bake in an oven 190°C/375°F/Gas Mark 5 for 20 minutes.

Serve warm or cold.

Serves 12 ***Preparation*** 10mins ***Cooking*** 20mins ***Calories*** 265 each ***Fat*** 3½g ea

blueberry
muffins

2 cups plain flour

$^1/_4$ cup sugar

3 tsp baking powder

$^1/_2$ tsp salt

1 cup milk

$^1/_3$ cup butter, melted

1 egg beaten

$^1/_2$ cup blueberries

Makes 10
Preparation 20mins
Cooking 25mins
Calories 193 each
Fat 4g each

1 Grease $^1/_3$-cup-size mufin tins or deep patty pans and set oven temperature at 200°C/400°F/Gas Mark 6

2 Sift flour, sugar, baking powder and salt together. Combine milk, butter and egg with a fork. Make a well in the centre of the flour and add milk mixture and the blueberries. Stir quickly with a fork, until dry ingredients are moistened. Do not beat. The batter will be lumpy. Put a large spoonful of batter into each muffin pan. Cups should be just more than half full. Use spoon which will hold the quantity of batter needed for each cup because for perfect muffins you should put in the batter in one lot.

3 Bake in a hot oven for 20-25 minutes or until golden. serve hot or warm with lashings of butter.

apple cinnamon

1 Preheat oven to 200°C/400°F/Gas Mark 6. Spray 12 small muffin pans with canola spray.

2 Put the pie apple in a bowl, stir in half the cinnamon and set aside.

3 Sift the flour, baking powder and remaining cinnamon into a large bowl, stir in the rolled oats and brown sugar. Make a well in the centre.

4 Put the milk, eggs, vanilla essence, oil and yoghurt in a jug and whisk to combine.

5 Pour the liquid ingredients into the well and mix until just combined - do not over mix - the mixture should still be lumpy. Over mixing will also make the muffins tough.

6 Half fill the muffin cups with the muffin mixture, place half a tablespoon of the apple mixture into each cup, then top with the remaining muffin mixture.

7 Sprinkle with the brown sugar and rolled oats. Bake for 25-30 minutes or until the muffins are risen and have started to come away from the side of the tin. Allow to cool for 5 minutes in their tins before turning out onto a wire rack to cool completely.

---

canola cooking spray

7oz/200g canned pie apple

1 tsp ground cinnamon

2¹/₂ cups plain flour

3 tsp baking powder

1 cup rolled oats

²/₃ cup brown sugar

13oz/370mL reduced fat milk

2 eggs, lightly beaten

1 tsp vanilla essence

2 tbsp safflower oil

3¹/₂ oz/100g thick, reduced fat vanilla yoghurt

2 tbsp brown sugar, extra

2 tbsp rolled oats, extra

Serves makes 12   **Preparation** 15mins   **Cooking** 25-30mins
Calories 230 each   **Fat** 4g each

muffins

mini
chocolate muffins

with mocha sauce

55g/2oz unsalted butter, diced, plus extra for greasing

55g/2oz plain chocolate, broken into pieces

2 medium eggs

85g/3oz superfine sugar

85g/3oz plain flour

$1/2$ tsp baking powder

30g/1oz cocoa powder, sifted, plus extra for dusting

For the mocha sauce

145g/145g plain chocolate, broken into pieces

85mL/3fl oz espresso or other strong, good quality coffee

145mL/5fl oz carton double cream

1 Preheat the oven to 350°F/180°C/Gas Mark 4. Grease a 12 cup muffin tray. Melt the chocolate and butter in a bowl set over a saucepan of simmering water. Put the eggs, sugar, flour, baking powder and cocoa powder into a bowl and beat for 1 minute, then beat in the melted chocolate and butter.

2 Spoon into the muffin tray, allowing one tablespoon for each cup. Bake for 15 minutes or until risen and firm to the touch.

3 Meanwhile, make the mocha sauce. Put the chocolate, coffee and 55mL/2fl oz of cream into a small pan and heat gently. Simmer for 1-2 minutes, until the sauce has thickened slightly. Keep warm.

4 Leave the muffins to cool on a wire rack for 5 minutes. Whisk the remaining cream until thickened, then spoon over the muffins together with the mocha sauce. Serve dusted with cocoa powder.

Note: You'll need a 12 cup, non-stick muffin tray for these mini muffins or, if you prefer, you can make large muffins and increase the cooking time to 25 minutes.

Serves *makes* 12 **Preparation** *10mins plus 5mins cooling*
Cooking *15mins* **Calories** *160* **Fat** *11g*

buttery

spice tea puffs

85g/3oz butter, softened

¹/₂ cup sugar

1 large egg

1¹/₂ cups flour

1¹/₂ tsps baking powder

¹/₄ tsp freshly grated nutmeg

¹/₂ cup milk

¹/₃ cup chopped walnuts or pecans

Topping

30g/1oz butter, softened

2 tbsps sugar

¹/₂ tsp cinnamon

1 Preheat oven to 180°C/350°F/Gas Mark 4 and butter 12 x ¹/₃ cup-size muffin pans.

2 In a bowl, beat together the butter and sugar until creamy, add the egg, beating well. Sift together the flour, baking powder and nutmeg, then add to the eggs along with the milk and half the nuts. Stir until just smooth, but do not beat the mixture.

3 Spoon the mixture into buttered muffins pans, sprinkle over the remaining nuts and bake in the preheated moderate oven for 20-25 minutes, or until pale golden.

Topping: While puffs are baking, put butter into a small bowl and mix sugar and cinnamon in a separate bowl. When puffs are cooked and while still hot, brush tops with butter then sprinkle over cinnamon sugar. Serve warm.

Serves 12
Preparation 20mins
Cooking 25mins
Calories 197 each
Fat 5g each

2 savoury muffins

cheddar
and pepper muffins

255g/9oz plain flour

1 1/2 tsp baking powder

1/2 tsp baking soda

1/2 tsp salt

1/4 tsp cayenne pepper

85g/3oz polenta

225g/8oz grated mature Cheddar cheese

6-8 spring onions with green tops, thinly sliced

1 small red pepper (capsicum), diced

55g/2oz butter

2 tbsp sugar

2 eggs

310mL/11fl oz buttermilk

1 Sift flour, baking powder, baking soda, salt and cayenne pepper into a bowl, add polenta, Cheddar cheese, spring onions and red pepper (capsicum) and mix well.

2 In a large bowl beat butter and sugar until creamy, add eggs and beat until smooth. Fold dry ingredients into creamed mixture alternately with buttermilk until just combined. Take care not to overmix.

3 Preheat oven to 220°/425°F/Gas 7. Spoon batter into eighteen greased 90mL/3floz capacity muffins pan and bake for 15-18 minutes or until cooked. Serve warm.

Serves *makes 18 muffins*
Preparation *20mins*
Cooking *20mins*
Calories *158 each*
Fat *4 1/2g each*

mini

sardine muffins

1 1/2 cups plain flour

2 tsp baking powder

1 tbsp lemon thyme
pinch paprika

1 egg

1/4 cup canola oil

3/4 cup milk

115g/4oz can sardines
in tomato sauce,
mashed

Serves *4*
Preparation *2 mins*
plus 2hrs chilling
Cooking *14mins*
Calories *219 each*
Fat *0.4g each*

1 Combine flour, baking powder, lemon thyme
and paprika in bowl. In separate dish mix
together the egg, oil and milk. Quickly and
lightly combine the dry and liquid ingredients.
Fold in the sardines. Spoon mixture into lightly
greased muffin pans or patty pans. Bake in an
oven at 200°C/400°F/Gas Mark 6 for 12-14
minutes or until golden. Serve warm.

mixed

mushrooms on

1 Halve any large mushrooms. Heat 2 teaspoons of the oil in a heavy-based frying pan, then add all the mushrooms, season lightly and fry over a medium to high heat for 5 minutes or until they start to release their juices.

2 Remove the mushrooms and drain on kitchen towels, then set aside. Add the rest of the oil and half the butter to the pan and heat until the butter melts. Add the garlic and stir for 1 minute.

3 Return the mushrooms to the pan, then increase the heat to high and fry for 5 minutes or until they are tender and starting to crisp. Stir in the remaining butter and 2 tablespoons each of parsley and chives, drizzle with the vinegar and season.

4 Mix the soft cheese with the remaining parsley and snipped chives. Split and toast the muffins. Spread the soft cheese mixture over the muffin halves and place on serving plates. Top with the mushrooms and garnish with the whole chives.

510g/18oz mixed mushrooms, including wild, oyster and shiitake

2 tbsp olive oil

salt and black pepper

30g/1oz butter

1 clove garlic, crushed

3 tbsp chopped fresh parsley

3 tbsp finely snipped chives, plus extra whole chives to garnish

2 tsp sherry vinegar or balsamic vinegar

4 tbsp low-fat soft cheese

3 English white muffins

Serves 6 **Preparation** 10mins **Cooking** 15mins **Calories** 177 each **Fat** 11g eac

herbed muffins

mushroom
muffins

2 cups plain flour

1 tbsp baking powder

55g/2oz fresh mushrooms, chopped

¹/₂ cup cooked brown rice

¹/₂ cup shredded tasty (mature Cheddar) cheese

1 tbsp parsley flakes

2 tsp chives, chopped

115g/4oz margarine, melted

255mL/9fl oz milk

1 egg, beaten

1 Sift flour and baking powder into a large bowl. Mix in mushrooms, rice, cheese and herbs.

2 Make a well in the centre of the dry ingredients. Add the remaining ingredients. Mix until just combined (see note).

3 Spoon mixture into greased muffin pans until three quarters full. Bake in the oven at 200°C/400°F/Gas Mark 6 for 25 minutes. Remove from pan. Cool on a wire rack. Serve hot or cold.

Note: Don't worry if not all the flour is incorporated as this gives muffins their characteristic texture. Sixteen strokes is usually enough when mixing.

Serves *makes 12*   **Preparation** *20mins*   **Cooking** *25mins*
Calories *195 each*   **Fat** *2g each*

2 eggs	
55mL/2fl oz cream	
1 bunch dill	
black pepper to taste	
30g/1oz Edam cheese, grated	
225g/8oz can tuna, drained and flaked	

tuna

puffs

Serves *makes 12*
Preparation *15mins*
Cooking *12mins*
Calories *64 each*
Fat *2g each*

1 Beat together the eggs and cream, season to taste with dill and black pepper. Fold in the cheese and tuna.

2 Place spoonfuls of the mixture into lightly greased muffin pans or patty pans.

3 Bake in an oven 200°C/400°F/Gas Mark 6 for 10-12 minutes or until puffed and golden. Serve hot or warm.

3

quick

breads

hot
brownies with white

1 Preheat the oven to 180°C/350°F/Gas Mark 4. Grease the sides and base of an 18cm/7in square cake tin. Beat the margarine and sugar in a bowl until pale and creamy, then beat in the egg, syrup, cocoa powder, flour and baking powder until it forms a thick, smooth batter. Stir in the nuts.

2 Spoon the mixture into the tin, smooth the top and bake for 35-40 minutes, until well risen and just firm to the touch.

3 Meanwhile, make the chocolate sauce. Blend the cornstarch with 1 tablespoon of the milk. Heat the rest of the milk in a saucepan, add the cornstarch mixture, then gently bring to the boil, stirring as the sauce thickens. Cook gently for 1-2 minutes.

4 Add the white chocolate, then remove from the heat and stir until it melts. Cut the brownies into 8 pieces and serve warm with the chocolate sauce.

Note: These brownies are delicious when they're cold, but when they're served straight from the oven with white chocolate sauce spooned all over them, they're absolutely fabulous!

85g/3oz soft margarine, plus extra for greasing

85g/3oz soft dark brown sugar

1 large egg, beaten

1 tbsp golden syrup

1 tbsp cocoa powder, sifted

55g/2oz wholemeal flour, sifted

$1/4$ tsp baking powder

1oz/30g pecan nuts or walnuts, chopped

White chocolate sauce

1 tbsp cornstarch

200mL/7fl oz full-fat milk

55g/2oz white chocolate, broken into small chunks

***Serves** 6 **Preparation** 15mins **Cooking** 40mins **Calories** 327 each **Fat** 4g each*

chocolate sauce

| 1 cup coconut |
| 2 cups unbleached bread flour |
| $1/2$ tsp salt |
| 1 tbsp baking powder |
| 1 cup milk |
| 1 egg, beaten |
| $1/2$ cup melted butter or peanut oil |
| 1 tbsp vanilla |
| $1/2$ cup sugar |
| 1 tsp superfine sugar, extra, for sprinkling |

toasted

coconut bread

1 To toast the coconut, place in a shallow baking pan in an oven preheated to 180°C/350°F/ Gas Mark 4. Bake for 5 minutes or until golden brown.

2 Mix together the flour, salt and baking powder. In a separate bowl, mix the milk, egg, oil, vanilla and sugar and add to the dry mix. Add coconut. Pour the batter into a well-oiled loaf pan and sprinkle with the superfine sugar. Bake at 180°C/350°F/Gas Mark 4 for 1 hour or until a tester comes out clean. Cool in pan for 10 minutes, then turn out onto a wire rack to cool.

Serves *4-6* ***Preparation*** *20mins*
Cooking *60mins plus 10mins cooling* ***Calories*** *2881 total* ***Fat*** *94g total*

lemon

quick bread

125g/4½oz butter, softened

½ cup sugar

2 large eggs, beaten

grated rind and juice of 1 lemon

¼ tsp cinnamon

½ tsp ground cilantro (coriander)

1½ cups unbleached bread flour

½ tsp salt

2 tsp baking powder

½ cup milk

1 Cream the butter and sugar until the mixture is light and fluffy. Add the eggs, one at a time, beating well after each addition. Add the grated lemon rind and juice, cinnamon and cilntro (coriander). Mix well.

2 Mix the flour, salt and baking powder in a bowl.

3 To the butter mixture add half of the flour mixture, then half of the milk. Repeat until all ingredients are combined.

4 When all ingredients are incorporated and the mixture is well mixed, pour into a well-oiled loaf pan and bake at 180°C/350°F/Gas Mark 4 for 45 minutes, or until a tester comes out clean. Cool in the pan for 10 minutes then turn out onto a wire rack.

Serves *4*
Preparation *25mins*
Cooking *45mins*
Calories *2272 total*
Fat *69g total*

fresh

strawberry scones

1 Preheat the oven to 220°C/425°F/Gas Mark 7. Put the flour, baking powder and salt in a large bowl and stir to mix. Lightly rub in the sunflower spread until the mixture resembles breadcrumbs.

2 Mix in the sugar and strawberries, then add enough milk to form a soft dough. Turn the dough out onto a floured surface, knead lightly, then carefully roll to a thickness of 2cm./³/₄in

3 Cut out 12 rounds, using a 5cm/2in pastry cutter, and place on a baking sheet. Brush with milk to glaze. Bake in the oven for 8-10 minutes, until well risen and golden brown. Transfer to a wire rack to cool.

Note: To give these traditional scones a warm, spicy flavour, add a teaspoon of ground cinnamon to the flour at the start of this recipe. Serve with crème fraîche and strawberries.

225g/8oz wholemeal flour

2 tsp baking powder

pinch of salt

55g/2oz sunflower spread

30g/1oz superfine sugar

100g/3½oz fresh strawberries, chopped

115mL/4fl oz half-fat milk, plus extra for glazing

***Serves** 4 **Preparation** 15mins*
***Cooking** 10mins **Calories** 104 each **Fat** 4g each*

wholemeal
raisin bread

1½ cups stoneground wholemeal flour

1½ cups unbleached bread flour

1½ tsp of baking soda

125g/4½oz butter, cut into cubes

1 cup golden raisins or sultanas

1 cup buttermilk

1 large egg

1 Mix the flours and soda and rub the butter in with fingertips, or use a food processor fitted with a metal blade and process until the flour resembles course breadcrumbs.

2 Add the golden raisins. Mix the buttermilk with the egg and sugar and add to the flour mixture. Pour the batter into a well-oiled loaf pan and cut a line down the centre of the batter. Bake at 180°C/350°F/Gas Mark 4 for 45 minutes, or until a tester comes out clean.

Serves 4-6
Preparation 20mins
Cooking 45mins
Calories 2979 total
Fat 68g total

country
cornbread

1 cup cornmeal
1 cup flour
2 tbsp sugar
1 tbsp baking powder
$^1/_2$ tsp salt
$^3/_4$ cup milk
$^1/_2$ cup sour cream
2 eggs
100g/3$^1/_2$oz melted butter

1 In a large mixing bowl, stir together all the dry ingredients. Mix the milk, cream, eggs and butter separately and blend well. Mix with the flour mixture just until combined.

2 Pour the batter into a well-oiled square cake pan, about 23 x 23cm/9 x 9in. Bake at 180°C/350°F/Gas Mark 4 for approximately 30 minutes until a tester comes out clean. Cut into squares or rectangles and serve warm.

Serves 4 **Preparation** *10mins* **Cooking** *30mins* **Calories** *2263 total* **Fat** *72g total*

sun-dried

dried tomato &

4 tbsp olive oil

2 tbsp sugar

2 large eggs

2 tsp ground garlic

1 1/4 cups buttermilk

2 1/2 cups unbleached bread flour

2 tsp baking powder

1/2 tsp baking soda

1 1/2 tsps salt

1 cup provolone cheese, or other sharp yellow cheese, grated

1/2 cup spring onions, thinly sliced

1/2 cup fresh parsley, chopped

1 tsp freshly ground black pepper

1/2 cup sun-dried tomatoes chopped

1 Mix the oil, sugar, eggs, garlic and buttermilk in a bowl until smooth.

2 In a separate bowl, mix the flour, baking powder, baking soda and salt together, then add the cheese, spring onions, parsley, pepper and tomatoes.

3 Add the buttermilk mix to the flour mix and stir until ingredients are combined. Do not over mix.

4 Pour the batter into a greased loaf pan and smooth the top with a wet spoon. Bake at 180°C/350°F/Gas Mark 4 for 50 minutes. Allow to cool for 10 minutes before removing from pan.

Serves *4-6* **Preparation** *30mins* **Cooking** *50mins plus 10mins cooling*
Calories *2578 total* **Fat** *35g total*

provolone quick bread

cheese
& bacon damper

3 tbsp margarine or butter
2½ cups flour
3 tsp baking powder
2 tsp parsley flakes
1 tsp chopped chives
1 cup grated tasty (mature Cheddar) cheese
2 rashers cooked bacon, finely chopped
1 egg
¾ cup milk

1 Rub the margarine into the flour and baking powder until mixture resembles coarse breadcrumbs.

2 Stir in parsley, chives, cheese and bacon, mix well.

3 Combine the egg and milk, stir into the dry ingredients and mix to a soft dough.

4 Turn dough onto a lightly-floured board and knead lightly.

5 Shape into a cob, cut a deep cross in the centre of the cob and place on a sheet of baking paper on an oven tray.

6 Bake in the oven at 200°C/400°F/Gas Mark 4 for 30 minutes or until hollow-sounding when tapped underneath.

7 Serve hot with a crock of butter on a buffet table, cut into small pieces.

Serves 6-8
Preparation 20mins
Cooking 30mins
Calories 2530 loaf
Fat 53g loaf

potato

scones

185g/6½ oz plain flour

1 tsp baking powder

½ tsp salt

125g/4½ oz margarine

2 eggs, beaten

100mL/3½fl oz milk

115g/4oz cold mashed potato

3 shallots, finely chopped

ground black pepper

flour, for kneading

butter, for spreading

Serves 6-8

Preparation 20mins

Cooking 30mins

Calories 225 each

Fat 3g each

1 Sift the flour, baking powder and salt together, then rub in the margarine. Beat the eggs and milk together and add to flour mixture to make a firm dough.

2 Add finely mashed potatoes, shallots and pepper. Stir through lightly. Turn onto a floured board or sheet of non-stick oven paper, knead, then roll out to 1cm/½in thickness. Cut into rounds and bake in 230°C/450°F/Gas Mark 8 oven for 30 minutes. Split open while hot and spread with butter and serve.

onion

flat bread

1 Slice the onions and sauté in the butter until transparent. Set aside.

2 Mix the flour, salt, pepper, sugar, baking powder and chives in a large bowl. In a separate bowl, mix 1 of the eggs with the milk. Add this to the flour mixture. Mix just until incorporated. Pour this batter into a well-oiled casserole or baking pan measuring approximately 30 x 20cm/12 x 8in.

3 Mix the onions with the remaining eggs and sour cream and mix well. Carefully spoon the onion mixture over the dough and bake at 180°C/350°F/Gas Mark 4 for 30 minutes, or until the custard is set and the bread is cooked through.

Serves 6-8
Preparation 30mins
Cooking 40mins
Calories 2608 total
Fat 80g total

6 brown onions
85g/3oz butter
2 cups unbleached bread flour
1 tsp salt
1/2 tsp freshly ground pepper
1 tsp sugar
1 tbsp baking powder
1/2 cup chives, chopped
3 large eggs
1 1/2 cups milk
1 cup sour cream

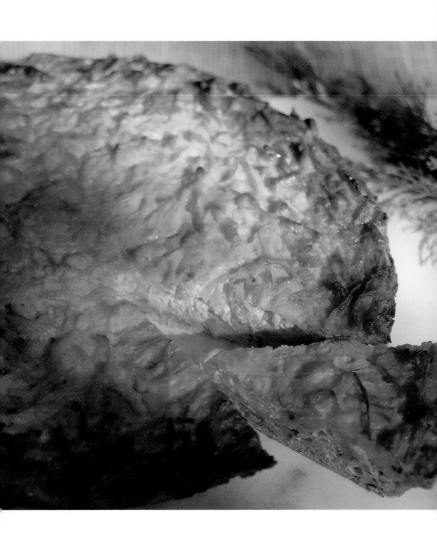

cream cheese

and apple scones

1 Preheat the oven to 200°C/400°F/Gas Mark 6. Grease a baking sheet.

2 Sift the flour, baking powder and a good pinch of salt into a bowl, then stir in the oatmeal, mustard powder and sugar. Rub in the butter using your fingertips until it resembles fine breadcrumbs. Stir in the cheese and apples and bind with just enough soured cream or buttermilk to make a soft but not sticky dough.

3 Roll out the dough on a floured surface to about 2cm/³⁄₄in thick and stamp out 8 scones, using a 6cm/2¹⁄₂in pastry cutter. Without overhandling the dough, press the trimmings together and roll out again to make more scones. Place on the baking sheet, brush the tops with soured cream or buttermilk and lightly dust with oatmeal. Bake for 15 minutes, then cool on a wire rack for a few minutes before serving.

Note: These scones bring together a blend of sweet and savoury. Try them with clotted cream.

50g/2oz butter, cubed, plus extra for greasing

200g/7oz plain flour

3 tsp baking powder

salt

50g/2oz fine oatmeal, plus extra for dusting

¹⁄₂ tsp English mustard powder

1 tsp superfine sugar

125g/4oz cream cheese, cut into 1cm/¹⁄₂in cubes

1 large or 2 small eating apples, peeled, cored and chopped into 5mm/¹⁄₄in pieces

4-5 tbsp soured cream or buttermilk, plus extra for glazing

Serves 10-12 scones   **Preparation** 20mins
Cooking 15mins   **Calories** 195 each   **Fat** 10g each

weights and measures

quick converter

Metric	Imperial
5mm	1/4 in
1cm	1/2 in
2cm	3/4 in
2 1/2 cm	1 in
5cm	2 in
10 1/2 cm	4 in
15cm	6 in
20cm	8 in
23cm	9 in
25cm	10 in
30cm	12 in

metric cups and spoons

Metric	Cups	Imperial
60mL	1/4 cup	2 fl oz
80mL	1/3 cup	2 1/2 fl oz
125mL	1/2 cup	4 fl oz
250mL	1 cup	8 fl oz
Metric	**Spoons**	
1 1/4 mL	1/4 teaspoon	
2 1/2 mL	1/2 teaspoon	
5mL	1 teaspoon	
20mL	1 tablespoon	

measuring liquids

Metric	Imperial	Cups
30mL	1 fl oz	
55mL	2 fl oz	1/4 cup
85mL	3 fl oz	
115mL	4 fl oz	1/2 cup
150mL	5 1/4 fl oz	
170mL	6 fl oz	2/3 cup
185mL	6 1/2 fl oz	
200mL	7 fl oz	
225mL	8 fl oz	1 cup
285mL	10 fl oz	
370mL	13 fl oz	
400mL	14 fl oz	
455mL	16 fl oz	2 cups
570mL	20 fl oz	
1 litre	35.3 fl oz	4 cups

oven temperatures

°C	°F	Gas Mark
120	250	1/4
140	275	1
150	300	2
160	325	3
180	350	4
190	375	5
200	400	6
220	425	7
240	475	8
250	500	9

measuring dry ingredients

Metric	Imperial
15g	$^1/_2$oz
20g	$^2/_3$oz
30g	1oz
55g	2oz
85g	3oz
115g	4oz
125g	4$^1/_2$oz
140g	5oz
170g	6oz
200g	7oz
225g	8oz ($^1/_2$lb)
255g	9oz
315g	11oz
370g	13oz
400g	14oz
425g	15oz
455g	16oz(1lb)
680g	1 lb 8oz
1kg	2.2lb
1$^1/_2$ kg	3.3lb

index